The Way Heaven Thinks

JOSEPH GIL

Cover design by Christian Wetzel

Published by: Coast Christian Fellowship
4000 Pacific Coast Highway
Torrance, CA 90505
www.coastchristian.org

CONTENTS

FORWARD to *The Way Heaven Thinks*

As the Executive Pastor in a large church in Southern California, I have seen a lot of Christian leaders come and go. Unfortunately, I can only name a handful that truly lived out Christ's charge to us as they died to themselves, picked up their cross daily and followed Him (Matt 16:24-25). Joe Gil is one if those rare men. As you'll see, His commitment to serving Christ above all else and then loving others unconditionally is lived out in the following pages.

It's easy to write about Christian character, it's another thing to live it. Once you open this book, you will be reading the reflections of a man that I would want in my foxhole. When the evil forces of the world attack, I want someone like Joe Gil by my side, covering my back, leading the way.

Isaiah responded to Gods call by declaring "here I am Lord, send me," (Isaiah 6:8). Like Isaiah, Joe is the consummate servant who is answering God's call. As long as I've known him, he's been fully immersed in living out Christ's commandment to love Him with all of his heart, his mind, his soul and his strength, and then others before himself (Matt 22:37-39).

As you read through *The Way Heaven Thinks*, I pray that you take the time to reflect on Joe's thoughts, absorb his teachings, meditate on his encouragements and put into action his challenges. And perhaps, one day, you too will hear the same words that I know the Lord will pronounce upon Joe, "Well done good and faithful servant."

May God bless you in your journey,

Dale Turner

Executive Pastor

Hope Chapel, Hermosa Beach, California

INTRODUCTION

I originally began writing this book to encourage associate pastors like myself in their support role. I see so many associates feel that when they become a senior pastor, they will arrive. This mindset makes it nearly impossible to be an excellent servant. I have seen many associates leave out of frustration too early and forfeit the blessing of inheritance. The truth is, there is no goal beyond serving. To serve is to arrive. I wanted to give a more complete viewpoint from God's perspective so that those in support roles would never feel incomplete or unimportant. Then I realized that there was a good chance that the entire Body of Christ could benefit from this book.

When I began my journey into the ministry, I had a very different idea of what I was getting into. I was set on learning the tricks of the trade and becoming a master at my skill. I thought I would be successful if I gained the knowledge and implemented the principles of other 'successful' ministers. I quickly found that I was way off. What I discovered was that if I wanted to be a successful leader, I desperately needed influence. Then the question came - how do I get it? Do I strive to find a better ministry model, scour the theology books for a better argument or does it come from another source?

Since I've begun asking these questions, I began to find that influence is given as a blessing from God as He trusts a person with His people. This was not something I could learn from a book or gain from a conference. It would only come as my heart was transformed to look more like His. In this book I share some of the key heart lessons I learned as I've grown in appreciation of Heaven's perspective of my life. My hope is that you too would begin to think like Heaven and experience the deep and lasting friendship that God has called us into. The goal is to raise up a company of servant leaders who reflect the core values of Jesus as we shepherd others into the Kingdom.

It is my prayer that after reading these pages, you will resemble Jesus more than you did before.

1. CHANGE YOUR PRAYERS

There was a season when I was frustrated with my role in the church I was serving. I felt as though there was a ceiling on my potential. My prayers seemed to be blocked by other people's decisions. You know how it is: you want something, and your excuse for being discontent is that you think God wants what you want too. I wanted "revival", and I felt that we were not getting it. These "unanswered prayers" were breeding frustration in me. I was certain that God felt the same way that I did, for of course He wants revival as well right?

One day in prayer I was pouring out my feelings to the Lord and He simply replied, "Change your prayers."

"What?!" I exclaimed.

He went on, "You are frustrated because you have an agenda that is not getting met. If you change your prayers according to *My* desire, you will never feel like you have a ceiling on you again." I heard the answer just like that. His voice shook me. The next thing He said was, "Ask to be more of a servant, a support to others and make it your goal to go lower." This was not a new concept to me, however, I knew that this call of God was a heavy one. We talk about going 'lower' but what does it really mean?

In Luke 9:46 a fight breaks out among the disciples about who is the greatest. Could you imagine discussing this with your buddies?

"Hey, Phil, I bet Jesus thinks I'm more anointed than you. I've cast out more unclean spirits than you, my sermons are more powerful and more people follow me."

"No way, Nate, I'm pretty certain my humility means more to Him than all of your works put together. Plus, I have a higher position than you in our denomination."

Haha, that would sound so obnoxious, wouldn't it? I found that I was that person. I was the one who was anxious to show my stuff and race into public ministry. But that wasn't all I found. I found that the reason I was in such a hurry was because my definition of success had been defined by a godless society. Although it is not popular to say these things out loud, it does not mean that our hearts are free from this attitude.

Jesus, knowing their thoughts, brings a little child forward and says *he* is the greatest. There is something about a child that reveals the striving heart of the adult. Children's minds are set on the opposite of striving for greatness. In their simplicity and innocence, their goals are actually more aligned with the things of God— relationship, love, joy. Their core values are actually closer to God's!

My kids often bring me back to reality and what's important. I can be so bent on getting something accomplished that I see their desire for attention as an obstacle. When I am frustrated with my kids, I know that my mind is set on productivity and striving, and I sense my Father reminding me to return to His rest.

I remember a time when I would be in such a hurry to get to work that I would be ready twenty minutes before I had to leave. I frequently checked my watch while I was playing with my kids which does not lend to a genuine interaction. I remember my wife used to say, "Why are you in such a hurry, you don't have to leave yet." God eventually got my attention and I realized that I was focused on what I needed to accomplish at the church while I was playing with them. It saddened me because I never want my kids to call my name three times before I snap back to the present moment. I consciously made an effort from that point forward to be present while I was at home. We all celebrated the day when I was so engrossed with building Legos that I was late for work!

If I can receive a little child, then I know my heart and mind are in the right place; I am rested, relaxed, and not striving to "be somebody." If I am focused on making a name for myself in the world in order to feel important, then a relationship with a child will seem futile. The greatest is defined so differently in heaven. For my real accomplishments are my relationships, the connections that I have, not the things I have built. Jesus' answer has been a perfect test for me. The qualities that God considers "great" is found in being child-like. The greatest or in other terms, 'success' is defined so differently in heaven.

In *The Empire Strikes Back*, Luke has an agenda to be a Jedi, not to defend the galaxy, but for his own purpose, to defeat Darth Vader out of revenge. So Luke travels in search of Yoda, the Jedi Master. When Luke finds him, Yoda does not reveal his identity but asks him to come and eat at his home. Luke becomes frustrated, so keen on obtaining his goal that he does not realize he is in the presence of the Jedi Master. It's not until Yoda reveals who he is to Luke that he responds with an interest and eagerness to learn. His attitude changed in an instant. His heart reflects my own heart and also reflects what is wrong with the Western culture today. We see people as opportunities to get instead of opportunities to give. God is calling us to adopt the goal of love, so that it does not matter who is in front of us, whether the president of the United States, a homeless person or a little child, we would love just the same.

Our hearts are revealed when a child is tugging on our shirt to read them a book. If we have a selfish agenda or an unhealthy desire for significance, this child does not have the potential to get us where we want to be, they become a "waste of time." We have opportunities all around us to love, like the socially awkward person at church who wants to talk to you and you find every excuse not to spend time with them.

Children have something that we need. Spending time with them can help simplify our complicated way of thinking. Children expose our ulterior motives in seeking the kingdom of God because children cannot give us anything. They cannot give us a promotion, a networking connection or a large donation for a new sanctuary. When a child asks us to come down to their level and sit on the floor with them, we must take the opportunity. Every time I do, that ugly part of my heart dies a little more. That part of me that uses opportunities and relationships for selfish gain is broken by being with a child. This leaves us with the next question, what is the definition of a successful ministry? What does a successful leader look like?

Your definition of success determines your out look on life, motivates your decisions and effects your behavior. In Matthew chapter 5, Jesus expounds on what a 'blessed' life is. Things like: being poor in spirit, mourning, gentleness, hungering for righteousness, being merciful, having a pure heart, being a peacemaker, and enduring persecution. These characteristics are not usually ones that we aspire to. They would not be the ones that we usually equate with 'success.'

We may know these verses intellectually but that does not mean that we are motivated by them. There are a variety of definitions of success at the core of each individual. Not the intellectual definition that people regurgitate when asked, that's not what I'm talking about. I'm referring to the core belief that was formulated from early teaching, experiences and relationships. For example; if you know someone who asked God for protection constantly, are suspicious of people they do not know, do not like to take risks, consider it a good day if nothing bad happens, and struggle with fear, then you can most likely conclude that their definition of a successful life would be to live a "safe" life. Safety is their core goal. These are the ones that focus on avoiding danger at all costs. In the parable of the talents (Matthew 25:14), this person would have buried their talent in the ground and would have gotten rebuked for it.

Being aware of your goals is very helpful because they determine when you are successful. If you are not aware of your core goal in life, how would you know when you have attained it? Also, and more importantly, knowing your goals is essential in order to change them. You have the power to choose the core goal of your life and you have the power to determine your goals for each situation.

Going back to what God said to me at the beginning of this chapter, He defined success for me, however when I tried to adopt this view everything contrary to this definition rose to the surface. My heart and my motives did not align with heaven's definition of success. Heaven's definition of success is found in Romans 8:29, *"For those whom He foreknew, He also predestined to become conformed to the image of His Son, so that He would be the firstborn among many brethren."* I'm supposed to look like Jesus, talk like Him and think like Him. When God is done with me I will resemble His Son. It gave me a whole new perspective. For there is ample opportunity for me to become more like Him.

Jesus' goal on earth was clear. He came as a servant. I quickly noticed that deep down, this was not my goal, but God was calling me to a higher standard. In the process what I have found is there is never a lack of opportunity to serve, to go lower. There may be people in the way of climbing to the top, but there is no one getting in the way of diving to the bottom! This concept radically shifted my thinking. If you would agree with me that Jesus lived a successful life, and His life resembled a servant, then you would also agree that our goal must change in order to match the qualities that are esteemed in heaven. I suppose Jesus would not be a good example of success in our modern Western society.

2. WHO IS THE GREATEST?

For who is greater, the one who reclines at the table or the one who serves? Is it not the one who reclines at the table? But I am among you as the one who serves.

- Luke 22:27

My boss at the first church I was employed, is one of the greatest men I know. He was much more than a boss, he was a mentor. He would say funny things about his role as a pastor, one I heard often was, "I am here to make the senior pastor look good." Usually when you hear that you think of somebody who is a kiss-up, a teacher's pet, a person who serves as a means of attracting attention to themselves for the purpose of promotion. Not this man. He did not want to preach, he never wanted to be a senior pastor and his personal dream was to move to another state with his family. He wasn't living out his dreams. You see, he put his dreams aside and made it his whole mission to assist and serve our senior pastor. His plan was to serve our senior pastor as long as he decided to be the senior pastor. He put his own dreams on hold until another person's dreams were fulfilled.

I found this amazing. How could someone base their whole life on another person's success? How could he be willing to lay down his own dreams to fulfill another's? What if the person he was helping failed? He was the first example I had seen of someone living out Jesus' words found in John 15:13 *"Greater love has no one than this, that he lay down his life for his friends."* It was by observing and interacting with this man that my thinking began to change. I began to understand heaven's mindset that we in the Western world have mostly forgotten, the mindset of placing someone else above ourselves.

Significance

Significance is not a terrible pursuit, for God wants to use us for great things. It is when we try to find our significance in the eyes of others instead of the eyes of God that gets us into an endless, empty pursuit. Those that try to find significance in the eyes of their fellow human beings will always come to a dead end. It will never fulfill the longing of the heart. Jesus did not have to search for the praise of people because He knew that He was significant in being a son, and that was enough. His approval came from the Father. With that security in place, Jesus was able to do and say whatever the Spirit led Him to without being encumbered by the fear of man. Whether people loved Him or hated Him, it did not matter. Many in our society do not have this security. Yet when our worth is found in the approval of God instead of man, it is easier to be led by the Spirit.

In 2000, a pastor asked me to assist him in planting a church. My wife and I felt led to go. As I prayed about it, God gave me a picture of Aaron holding up Moses' arms in battle. I was being called to assist him and give him strength as Aaron had to Moses. It wasn't until I set my heart to be a support to him and his dream, that I realized how self-centered I was. It seemed like selfish ambitions began to pop up everywhere as soon as I began to embrace a servant role. My goal was not only to have my actions supportive, but that I would do it from my heart as well. I had several instances when I was frustrated with his decisions because they went against my hidden personal dreams. I learned in the process that most of my frustrations revealed a personal agenda that was not being met. With every instance, God gently redirected the judgments of others toward my own heart.

There was nothing wrong with my dreams, but I began to see something more, something heavenly. I saw in Jesus that there was another way to think. To lay down my personal, even God given dreams to serve. I wanted to see what it would produce. If it was good enough for Jesus, then it was something to go after.

So I dove into this position instead of backing away from it. I wanted to see what else would come to the surface. I decided to fully surrender my life for someone else's dreams. It was kind of an experiment. I submitted my heart and future to another human being. *An imperfect human being.* I wish I could tell you that it has been all joy and no pain, but I would be lying. My senior pastor's choices were not my choices. I learned a lot about unity and serving, amongst other things. Every time I submitted and forsook my own agenda, selfish ambition died, because I intentionally killed it. By serving, layers of selfishness died and every layer that was gone produced something I never imagined, freedom. I experienced freedom from a self-protecting, broken heart that was scared to love.

In John chapter 6, Jesus had a pretty large following, and if he had had our Western mindset, he would have been concerned about keeping it. Instead, he said to the people, *"If you want to follow Me, you will have to eat My flesh and drink My blood."* John 6:56. At this point, many left. Jesus does not give an explanation or try to get them to come back. He then asked the small group remaining, *"Do you want to leave too?"*

Not what you would call a sermon that "attracts" people, and definitely not a move that would make it to our church growth manuals. We often make it easy to follow and hard to leave; Jesus made it hard to follow and easy to leave. It seems that Jesus was after something other than the goals of the Western church. It would be important for us to discover and adopt His way of thinking.

John the Baptist

In Matthew 11:11 Jesus described John the Baptist as the greatest born of a woman. Everything Jesus said is important to me. So when I read that Jesus called John the greatest human being ever born, I was very curious to know what he was so impressed with. John did not raise the dead, heal the sick, or perform signs and wonders. Nevertheless, somehow he possessed the key element that caught the eye of the Creator of the universe. I want to catch His eye like that!

As I began to study the life of John, I realized that my qualifications to define a person as "successful" differ from those of the Son of God. My new revelation was that those who do the greatest spiritual accomplishments on earth will not necessarily get the greatest reward. Men and women who have giant ministries may not be the greatest in the kingdom. In fact, those that are considered the greatest on earth, even in religious circles, may not be looked at the same from heavens point of view.

John the Baptist was one who obviously caught Jesus' attention. Interestingly, John's life was not about himself. The meaning and focus of his life was wrapped up in another, his friend. He was not concerned about the praise of others but only to prepare the way for someone he loved. Those that will have the greatest positions in heaven will be those that listen and follow closely to the Lord. Those that follow His leading. This may look different than our idea of a successful life in ministry. For God is not looking at the results, He is looking for a heart like John the Baptist, who, out of crazy love, would do anything and go anywhere for his savior.

Jesus addresses the mentality that many have today, that 'successful' people are the ones that produce the most results. It says in Matthew 7:21-24, *"Not everyone who says to me, 'Lord, Lord,' will enter the kingdom of heaven, but only he who does the will of My Father who is in heaven. Many will say to Me on that day, 'Lord, Lord, did we not prophesy in Your name, and in Your name drive out demons and perform many miracles?' Then I will tell them plainly, 'I never knew you. Away from Me, you evildoers!.' Therefore everyone who hears these words of Mine and puts them into practice is like a wise man who built his house on the rock."*

Many times I have asked the Lord to send me to a distant country as a missionary, or to plant a church in a remote town. He has again and again made it clear that I am to serve the senior pastor at my local church in my hometown. I have to be honest with you and say that what I do is not my first choice. Nor is it my second. I have my own list of things that I have asked for over the years. It is my own garden of Gethsemane experience – "Not my will but Yours." That may sound depressing unless you're like John the Baptist and find your joy in one thing: doing *His* will. That was also the number one joy of Jesus. He said that His "food" was to do the will (or desire) of the One who sent Him, and to accomplish His work, (John 4:34). I do not pretend that all I want is what God wants. Many of my goals are not God's, but I find that I am more in unity with the Holy Spirit when I serve Him rather than serve myself. I experience more fruit like joy, peace and love.

My hometown is a nice suburb in Southern California. We have great weather, we are close to our relatives and it is a safe, clean neighborhood. Even though it is where the Lord has planted us, I often times feel like I am not giving up enough, or sacrificing my life to answer the call to make disciples in third world countries. The enemy whispers that I need to accomplish more, reach more people and give up every comfort in order to please God. It is tempting to prove to others that I am "doing" something amazing for the Lord like risking my life in a remote jungle or in a dangerous city. But if I prophesy, heal the sick and raise the dead in the name of Jesus, but don't do as He leads, I'm afraid that when I stand before Him I will hear, "I never knew you." My life may not look like it is accomplishing much, but I can be confident in the fact that I have obeyed the voice of my One Love.

It may be that my job is to raise up the next Billy Graham. It may be that I am to serve another man in making his life more successful than it would have been if I was not there. It is not for me to determine what I accomplish, it is my job to know Jesus first, and follow Him wherever He goes. Our flesh is attracted to works, especially those that others can see, to feel important, but according to heaven, laying down one's life for another is the greatest act anyone can do. Jesus said it best in *Matthew 20:28, "the Son of Man did not come to be served, but to serve, and to give His life a ransom for many."*

When we have heaven's perspective, our love for others is so strong that we get lost in a pursuit to see them succeed. It is in this pursuit, it is in this heart, that we can accomplish much. This was why God took notice of John the Baptist and if I want Him to take notice of me then I must function in the same spirit.

Love

"If I speak with the tongues of men and of angels, but do not have love, I have become a noisy gong or a

clanging cymbal. If I have the gift of prophecy, and know all mysteries and all knowledge; and if I have all faith, so as to remove mountains, but do not have love, I am nothing. And if I give all my possessions to feed the poor, and if I surrender my body to be burned, but do not have love, it profits me nothing." – 1 Corinthians 13:1-3.

Love is a great goal. It fulfills so many of God's desires. However love for others is not the highest goal. It is not guaranteed that if you live a life of love, that you will be considered successful on this earth. There are many organizations that function out of a motivation of love and compassion. When Jesus' ministry first began he healed many in a town called Capernaum. The next morning, as wind of this news spread throughout the town, there were many more looking for Jesus. No doubt they had ailments and sick children. *"His disciples found Him, and said to Him, 'Everyone is looking for You.' He said to them, 'Let us go somewhere else to the towns nearby, so that I may preach there also; for that is what I came for.'"* – *Mark 1:37,38*. With crowds in need of the healing touch of Jesus, it must have been tempting for Him to stay, but Jesus was moved by something greater.

What is greater than love? What could be greater than compassion? In this story we see that Jesus was moved, not by the need of the crowd, but by the direction of His Father. This marked John the Baptist, it marked Jesus' life and it is to mark our lives. For to partner with the Father's desire on the earth in each moment is the ultimate thrill and success in life.

3. MY LIFE BELONGS TO ANOTHER

Have you ever heard a teaching about tithing in which the preacher comments that you should give your money and your time? This mindset is a funny Western way of getting people to ease into the Christian life. It is as if pastors have made it comfortable for people to enter in, as if they want to make it palatable. I have also heard them throw in teachings like "you can't out-give God." Teachings like these cause the church to dry up because in these teachings the standard for a follower of Christ has become depressingly low. The message has become, in essence, give God some of **your** time and money. The foundation of this message is off track, and we have therefore ended up with a people that have failed to reach their potential or their world.

What is off about this mindset is that we have bought into the lie that the money and time we possess are **ours**. The truth is that when a person decides to follow Jesus, they *leave* everything else behind. "Picking up your cross and following Him" is not and should not be an easy decision. Paul said in Galatians 2:20, *"I have* *been crucified with Christ and I no longer live, but Christ lives in me."* We in Western churches tend to find ourselves with teaching and standards that are way below par. In an attempt to encourage the body of Christ to give, we have created a self-centered church. Paul said in Romans 12 that we are to give ourselves as a "living sacrifice." That means that our lives are no longer ours. Our money is no longer ours. Our time is no longer ours. We have been bought with a price. Well, that's only *if* you have surrendered your life to Christ.

The reason why this is such an important part of the gospel is that we have robbed the church from experiencing true resurrection life. In Romans 6 it is clear that the abundant life is gained through the act of being crucified with Christ. Many Christians are not walking in the fullness of life because they have not identified with the death of Christ. Many shy away from the promise, "If you lose your life you will find it." It is sadly the fault of teachers that have been so motivated by church growth that they have allowed their teaching to be a tool to attract people.

It is evident that it was not Jesus' goal to make people feel comfortable. As I said before, Jesus made it hard for people to follow him and easy for them to leave, but we make it easy to get into the church and hard for people to leave. In Hindu and Muslim countries, when a person becomes a Christian, they give up their life. They most likely will lose their job, their friends, their family and many times even their physical life. In such places, the self-centered life ends with the decision to follow Christ. Not so here in the West. Don't get me wrong, I value the freedoms we have, I love my country and am glad to live here. I feel at times so blessed it is like I have won the lottery! However this comfort has a tendency, if you are not aware, to cause spiritual poverty.

A young missionary to Uganda, Katie Davis, in her book *Kisses from Katie* wrote,

> *People often ask if I think my life is dangerous, if I am afraid. I am much more afraid of remaining comfortable. Matthew 10:28 tells us not to fear things that can destroy the body but things that can destroy the soul. I am surrounded by things that can destroy the body. I interact almost daily with people who have deadly diseases, and many times I am the only person who can help them. I live in a country with one of the worlds largest-running wars taking place just a few hours away. Uncertainty is everywhere. But I am living in the midst of the uncertainty and risk, amid things that can and do bring physical*

destruction, because I am running from things that can destroy my soul: complacency, comfort, and ignorance. I am much more terrified of living a comfortable life in a self-serving society and failing to follow Jesus than I am of any illness or tragedy. Jesus called His followers to be a lot of things, but I have yet to find where He warned us to be safe.

In Mark 8:31-38, Jesus tells his disciples that he must suffer and die. Peter rebukes Jesus for talking this way. Jesus in turn rebukes Peter with these words: *"Get behind me Satan, for you are not setting your mind on God's interests, but man's."* Did Jesus use the name of our enemy to describe Peter's position? Wow, some pretty strong words from a friend! Peter's thinking was about self–preservation. Jesus goes on to tell his disciples that if they want to follow Him they must pick up their cross. In present-day terms, that's like saying you must embrace lethal injection if you want to be Jesus' student. Basically, Jesus is telling His disciples that they must think differently. He didn't say we must think about other things, because it is not *what* we are thinking about that is wrong, it is the *way* we are thinking. Therefore we need a change in the way we think, or to put it in Paul's words, we must renew our minds.

The book of James says, *"Who is wise and understanding among you? Let him show it by his good life, by deeds done in the humility that comes from wisdom. But if you harbor bitter envy and selfish ambition in your hearts, do not boast about it or deny the truth. Such 'wisdom' does not come down from heaven but is earthly, unspiritual, of the devil. For where you have envy and selfish ambition, there you find disorder and every evil practice"* James 3:13-16.

Did James say "of the devil"? Sounds kind of like his half brother Jesus, who said to Peter "Get behind me Satan!" This brings up a question, is there a way of thinking that is in line with our enemy? Yes, It is selfish thinking. Thinking about ourselves is a lot worse than we realize. The Satanic Bible is centered around one theme: "Do as thou wilt." Self-centered thinking makes the devil feel at home. There are two opposing mindsets, one set on serving self, and one set on serving others. It may seem as though we would be more happy and more fulfilled meeting our own needs, but Jesus shows us another way.

The opposite way is that of Jesus, *"Who, being in very nature God, did not consider equality with God something to be grasped, but made Himself nothing, taking the very nature of a servant, being made in human likeness. And being found in appearance as a man, He humbled Himself and became obedient to death—even death on a cross!"* Phil 2:6-8. This mindset is actually wisdom from heaven: to give your life, not to save it.

This is how God actually thinks!

It is not a way to think until you reach heaven, or a way of getting a good reward. It is the permanent way of thinking in heaven. I'm sure you've heard the saying that God's kingdom is an upside-down kingdom. Actually, *ours* is the one that is upside-down. *God's is right-side-up*.

Satan's way is to get you to set your mind on man's interests, or 'earthly' interests, to keep you from giving your life, to save yourself. He wants you to live your life and make decisions based on self-preservation and worse, self-promotion. Jesus had his mind set on giving his life for another. Why should we think any other way?

A mind set on God's interests does not focus on self. Instead, it focuses on how I can use my life to benefit someone else. This is not so you will be great in heaven; this mindset *is* great in heaven! It's the value system of heaven. It's the way they think up there!

4. SELF PROTECTION IS CONTRARY TO LOVE

Ever feel like you have a goal, maybe even a God-given goal for your life, and it continues to be elusive? Are there circumstances that refuse to change, or obstacles that you just cannot overcome? Maybe there are people standing in the way of that God-given dream that God has called you to follow.

I've noticed lately that one of the blockages to loving others is a fear that I will lose my life. What I mean by lose my life can be as simple as losing an hour listening to someone who I would rather not, or maybe a groups of friends are going to lunch after church and you notice someone in need. There is a big one for me though; it comes in the form of supporting another in their passions. Something rises up in me, it is the questions about my own path, fulfilling my own journey. What if I support this leader's vision, pour my time and energy into fulfilling this person's goals and in the end miss the opportunity to fulfill my own calling? In fact, when we choose leaders, what percentage of the motivation for choosing is based on how that leader can get me to where I want to go?

There was a time when my senior pastor's life was in a desperate place. The temptation for all of us was to jump ship. When I began to explore the reasons for leaving the church, I had all kinds of logical, even Biblical reasons that made sense. However, there was another reason under it all. It was a deep fear that this organization was going to plateau or worse, fail with me on board. My motives were based on selfish ambition. For if this ship was sinking, my ambitions where going to sink as well. I didn't want to waste any years supporting something, or someone that could not further my own ministry. I was sick to my stomach when I realized how self-serving my approach to ministry was. I was fearful of missing out on my own life and future. It was a fear that I had to deal with, a fear that had to die.

The definition of love that Jesus spoke of became painfully clear to me at that cross-road, *"Greater love has no one than this, that one lay down his life for his friends."* John 15:13. Ouch, would I be able to turn my back on all that God had promised me, all that He had put in my heart, to be there for a friend, that friend being my senior pastor? Could I face the reality that my life could end up in a disaster, standing by him, with no guarantee that things would turn out well? That was some serious dying right there! When you think about it, that is the attitude Jesus took with us, and yes, in the Father's eyes, my life would be a great success. A great success because that was true love, and a great success because I knew it was what Jesus was asking of me. *"This is My commandment, that you love one another, just as I have loved you. Greater love has no one than this that one lay down his life for his friends. You are My friends if you do what I command you."* John 15:12-14.

At the end of the Gospel of John, when Jesus meets the disciples at the seashore after His resurrection, He tells Peter to follow Him. In response Peter asks, what about John? Jesus says don't worry about John, what does that matter to you? Just follow Me, Peter.

There is a simplicity to following Jesus that brings peace. Every one of us has our own journey, and we must walk it out with Jesus. I can't walk out your destiny, and you cannot walk out mine. You may feel like people are keeping you from your destiny, but another person's choices cannot control what God has ordained for your life. Many times we get frustrated with people and their choices because we feel that their choices create a ceiling to our destiny. This sense of frustration reveals that we have an agenda that is not in alignment with God's ways. Your end goal may be in alignment, however you are not allowing God to work it out His way.

Saul was not following God when he tried to kill David, yet it did not thwart God's plan for David's life. In fact, God left Saul in charge for thirteen years after He rejected him as king of Israel and anointed David instead. God used every action of Saul's to ensure David's success as a king. Saul's actions actually assisted in the success of David's destiny. This may be speaking to *your* circumstance. I do not know if you have a Saul over you, but I do know that God wants to take the Saul *out of* you. God uses our 'Sauls' to make us into 'Davids.'

Anytime you have your eyes set on a person instead of God, you will be frustrated. No human being can get you where God wants you to go, and no human being can keep you from where God is taking you. The only block in you reaching your full potential and destiny is your lack of surrender to God's path to getting you there. In His timing we are raised up. If you feel any sense of frustration in this process, then there may be an agenda in your heart that is not God's agenda.

This also works in reverse. You may be a leader frustrated with those under your care. Moses struck the rock in Numbers 20 because he viewed the people as a roadblock to his destiny of entering the Promised Land. They were fearful about entering the land, plus they had a bad habit of grumbling about his leadership. He got frustrated with the people, called them rebels and struck the rock instead of speaking to it as God had instructed him. He misrepresented God to the people, and as a result God kept him from entering the Promised Land. The very thing that Moses had condemned the people of Israel for was what he himself was now guilty of, and in the end he had no one but himself to blame for not being able to meet his God-given dream.

Anytime we look to a human being—be it a spouse, a friend or even a pastor—as the means to entering into our personal destiny, we will be frustrated and disappointed. Likewise, anytime a pastor looks to the congregation as his ticket to the Promised Land, it will lead to frustration. Each person must hear the words "Follow Me" from Jesus for themselves, and we must each rely on Him to set the course. We cannot control anyone but ourselves.

Very often God prepares people in a secret place, through small tests of obedience, and sadly, many people fail to see that it is the small things that are significant in God's eyes. As 2 Chronicles 16:9 says, *"the eyes of the Lord range throughout the earth to strengthen those whose hearts are fully committed to him."* How do I prove that I am fully committed to Him? Abraham was tested when God asked him to sacrifice Isaac, Joseph was tested in jail, David was tested as a shepherd and when they had passed the test God raised them up to positions of great influence. Be careful not to mistaken God's testing ground as an obstacle to your destiny. Be faithful with little, and God will give you charge over more.

What are you most aware of?

Have you ever seen someone completely focused? Whatever it is, whether in spiritual things or in things in other aspects of life, their enthusiasm causes everyone within a ten-foot radius to get excited about the same thing. A focused individual is inspiring at the very least. What you are passionate about, or most aware of, you release to the world around you, whether positive or negative.

We realized as a pastoral staff that in our services we were so busy running the details of the service that we had no awareness of God's heart for His people. We were most 'aware' of the mechanics of the service, and not very aware of the Holy Spirit or how He wanted to lead us. We decided to raise up a group of lay pastors that were capable of running the services while we focused on Jesus in worship. As we did this, whenever anyone of us took the pulpit, we were most aware of God and were therefore able to release the things of God to the congregation.

When you find yourself in a church setting, what are *you* most aware of? Our attention can often wander to things like; music style, the attire of the singers, the way others are worshipping around us or even our own appearance. In the past I have at times found myself asking God, "What do you have for me? What is my destiny?" Our prayers often reveal what our focus is. I have realized that these prayers are self-focused. The most effective pursuit, the question we should be asking, is this: "Lord, what do you want to have happen in this service, and how can I help?"

I have often fallen into the trap of being focused on my spiritual and physical promotion, which hinders me from being aware of what God is doing. Thus, I become unaware of what God wants to release and what our people so desperately need. I have missed it because my eyes and my thoughts were set on something nowhere near to what God was thinking about. Self promotion is so far away from God's interests. Jesus never promoted Himself, nor was He concerned about making a name for Himself. He was concerned with what His Father was doing in every moment. He said that only did what He saw His Father doing. This meant that He was constantly 'looking' or focused on His Father at all times.

Intimacy

The Bible tells us about great people used by God to change the world. One common denominator I see in all of them is that their focus was on God. Every significant character in the Bible did not come into significance by focusing on significance. They became significant by obeying God, often times reluctantly. Their one goal was, as the apostle Paul wrote in Philippians 3, *"I want to know Christ."* Centuries before, David had also expressed this same desire: *"One thing I ask of the LORD, this is what I seek: that I may dwell in the house of the LORD all the days of my life, to gaze upon the beauty of the LORD and to seek Him in His temple"* Psalm 27:4.

We sing about this, we often pray about it, but how many of us really have intimacy with God as our first priority? If your number one goal is intimacy with God, you already have it. The veil has been torn! You do not need a higher position to seek His face. He is the same to the Jew and the Gentile, men and women, young person and old, and He is definitely the same towards the pastor, the church elder and the newborn Christian. You do not need to know your destiny to know God better. By Christ's death on the cross, we have complete access to the Father's presence. If He is your true goal, then you will not be frustrated with the roadblocks to your ministry and growth.

What will a position give you? Do you think you can love people more? Evangelize better? Heal the world? Instead of trying to gain a platform in order to tell the world about Jesus, why not just start telling the world about Jesus? Why not just start loving the world from where we are? Love the ones in front of you. If your motives and actions are in alignment with the

Father's, He will exalt you. His desire is to make Himself known, and if His nature is found in you, He will display you to the nations.

We must have a clear understanding what our job is and what is God's. Our job is to humble ourselves. His job is to exalt us, not the other way around. Nothing can stop you from reaching your goals with God because there is no ceiling for you. Position is simply a "bait" that leads away from real breakthrough. Love like Jesus loved and allow God to give you a platform in His time. Allow *God* to lift you up. He has no problem exalting people, especially when they are humble. *"Therefore humble yourselves under the mighty hand of God, that He may exalt you at the proper time"* 1 Peter 5:6. It is our job to humble ourselves, it is His job to exalt us.

If you haven't already done this, you might want to take a moment right now and decide for yourself what you really want, significance or Jesus, because at times in your life, these two goals will be diametrically opposed. There is a time coming when God is going to pour out His Spirit and He will be choosing leaders who have the purity of heart to be able to steward what is most precious to Him...people.

5. DEPENDENCY IS THE GOAL

I wish God would tell me what is going to happen in the next five years. It sure would make tough seasons easier. I'm convinced that difficult seasons in life are difficult because we do not know the outcome. We have to depend on the Holy Spirit our comforter step by step. During one particular season I was whining to Him and said, "I can't wait until this is over." Then I heard, "Over?" Then it hit me. God cherishes the seasons when we are most dependent on Him. He thoroughly enjoys the daily conversations, the constant checking in, the continuous dependency and emotional support. This is His idea of a good time! Why? Because He wants me to suffer? No, because to Him, relationship is the most valuable commodity. He longs for us to stop and talk. His desire is that we are deeply connected. His will is to be one with us (See John 17).

My old way of thinking was: when my life is set on a fixed course, when I have all the wisdom to know what to do in each situation, and when I am in charge of the church, then I will experience freedom. On the contrary true freedom does not come from being in charge of your life. True freedom is found in putting Jesus in charge of your life. The Bible says that Jesus is the Head of the Church, therefore the most effective leaders are the best followers.

When I was a newly hired pastor, I functioned out of a desperate reliance on the voice and direction of the Spirit, hoping not to make mistakes. I was so afraid of messing up the responsibility I had been given, I checked with God multiple times before I made a move. As I gained wisdom, the temptation arose in me to function out of my wisdom and past experience – and, as a result, I missed the direction of the Spirit! Somewhere I stopped checking with Him and used my intellect to determine direction. I began to make decisions based on what worked before. Wisdom is valuable, but to rely on wisdom more than the Spirit's leading is dangerous because God does not always do things the same every time. After all, God's goal is dependence, not independence.

God blesses us because of our hunger and obedience to the Spirit's leading. It is actually the best place to be: constant reliance on the Spirit and lack of wisdom is *better* than functioning from a place of wisdom and principle (which is where most people are trying to reach). Why? Everything we need is found in Him. All the wisdom and the knowledge in the world is no substitute for being led by the Spirit of God! I am convinced that I do not need more answers; I need more of Jesus.

One of the warnings that Jesus gave His disciples while He was on earth was to beware of the "yeast of Herod." The yeast of Herod represents a political spirit that seeks to gain leverage and influence by using others. It forms cliques and tries to gain votes. This spirit drives pastors and leaders to buddy-up to those with influence, considering it a waste of time to love those that cannot further their rise to power. The drive to climb the political ladder in the American church is so strong that Jesus' influence has been reduced to a tagline at the end of our prayers.

A classic case of the yeast of Herod, of choosing significance over obedience, is found in I Samuel 15: 30 when Saul had lost the approval of God, yet he still sought the approval of man. Then he (Saul) said, *"I have sinned; but please honor me now before the elders of my people and before Israel, and go back with me, that I may worship the Lord your God."* Saul wanted the prophet Samuel to make an appearance with him in front of the nation of Israel, so that he would appear to have favor with God, even though God had already rejected him as king. He should have been more concerned about being rejected by God than by the people, but his concern was to save face with the people. Who knows, if Saul would have repented to God at that moment, God may have reversed His opinion of Saul. Saul tragically was more concerned with what the people thought about him.

As we've seen earlier, Moses' life turned from focusing on God to focusing on the progress of His people, which caused him to strike the rock and lose his inheritance. Moses' frustration grew as his perspective changed. He began to focus on the fact that God's people might keep him from entering into the Promised Land. So instead of serving them, as God had called him to do, he saw them as a barrier to his desired destination.

Like Moses, many ministers strike the Rock today. In other words, they attack Jesus (The Rock) in prayer because their goals are not being met. An example of 'attacking' Jesus in prayer is inquiring of God in a way that puts the blame on Him for the congregations shortcomings. The people are not growing fast enough, they are not producing enough fruit, or are not serving enough. We imply the question directed towards God, "When are *You* going to do something about this?" We end up striking the Rock out of frustration. When Jesus charged Peter to lead and shepherd the new church, He used words that are not found too often in our church leadership manuals: "Feed my lambs." People are not numbers to be counted so that ministers can say how big their congregation is; they are to be fed and nurtured as a shepherd tends his lambs. It is a ministry of love.

When we build our ministries upon the Rock, its success is based upon our obedience to Christ. At the end of the day, we are to be content with the simple fact that we pleased our heavenly Father. When we evaluate our ministries based upon their success, we lose sight of who we are living for and may become frustrated. When this happens, *instead of our ministry being a tool for the Lord, the Lord becomes a tool for our ministry.* This can happen very subtly. God can become the resource to get us where we want to go. However, when our lives are built upon the Rock, then it is our joy to serve the body out of love for Jesus, and our gaze is to be upon Him, not on the congregation or the results.

In an environment where the political spirit rules, decisions are made based on how many will follow. Relationships are formed based on who can profit you the most. The problem with having the political spirit functioning in a church is that everyone is influenced by it, and everyone ends up thinking the same way. Mentality and motives are often shaped from the top down. So we as leaders create a culture where everyone is obsessed about evaluating the church leadership based on who can best fulfill their personal agenda. The people fall into this temptation instead of focusing on how their talents and resources can best propel the church forward. Everyone is jockeying for position. Service is talked about as a virtue but when there is an opportunity to serve no one feels "called." When there is an opportunity to love someone who has nothing to offer, for some reason everyone is busy.

We must wage a war against this political spirit, this yeast of Herod. How we do that is to attack it by the opposite spirit, the Spirit of Christ, who gave up His position in heaven to serve, not to be served. Let that mindset be the influence that motivates us.

6. DYING IS THE PATHWAY TO LIFE

"I tell you the truth unless a kernel of wheat falls to the ground and dies, it remains only a single seed. But if it dies, it produces many seeds." **John 12:24**

I have a friend named Dan who has been in missions for a few decades. While he was in Iran he was taken into custody and accused of being a spy. He was then incarcerated for nine weeks, interrogated and beaten every one of those days. At the first public prayer meeting at his home church, his mom prayed this prayer – "God do not take my son out of prison until all your purposes are fulfilled in him." Wow! Her faith and trust in the Lord to me is incredible. She saw this horrible situation as an opportunity and asked God to make the most out it.

Dan survived the ordeal. The time in prison accomplished something radical in him that continues to touch lives throughout the globe today. There a pathway to your destiny in God, and this path usually involves a death at some point, to yourself and to your dreams. Abraham was called to sacrifice his son, the very person that would fulfill what God had promised he would be: a father of many nations. Why would God do such a thing? Why would He put a dream in your heart and then test you by taking it away?

I think that one of the biggest fears in life is that the dreams in our hearts were not put there by God and that we will never fulfill them. We feel afraid because if they are only *our* dreams then it would be disobeying God to go after them. When God asks us to lay our dreams down, it would be tempting to think that He is not for those dreams. This is not why God calls us to die to our dreams. He asks us to sacrifice our 'Isaacs' for a different reason.

God brings us to a point of sacrificing our dreams because He wants to make sure that we will choose Him over what He has called us to. If we cannot reach this point, then that dream, that ministry, that job, will become our god. And what is the use gaining the whole world and yet losing our soul? The pathway to our destiny includes, at some point, the call to die. Even Jesus had to say no to His God given destiny. In the wilderness when He was tempted by Satan, He was shown all the kingdoms of the earth. Satan said He could have them if He would only bow down. It was Jesus' goal and destiny to have the nations, but bowing before Satan was the wrong way to get it. Jesus had to say no to His dreams in that moment. It was a test. The kingdoms were to be gained by dying, not bowing.

What is this thing about dying? Some make it a lifestyle and a goal. Their whole Christian life becomes about dying to self. They have contests about who fasts the most, who is the poorest or who is facing the most persecution, as if that were the measure of God's favor! In some circles, dying to self becomes the goal of their spirituality instead of a transitional pathway to destiny. God wants life for us and He tells us how to get there, *through* death. The word 'through' means that there is an ultimate goal on the other side. It is through losing our life that we find it, but the goal is still to find it, not stop at losing it. As far as God is concerned, the goal is not death but life. Our minds need renewing if this is our view of God's ways; He is better than we think. God has put dreams in our hearts, however, we often think that the way to get there is by gaining position, gaining knowledge, gaining followers, gaining power, gaining, gaining, gaining. On the contrary, it is only through losing our life that we gain, and when we are weak, He is strong! Sadly many churches in America are still trying to accomplish God's will with the world's strategies.

Maybe somewhere we got the idea that our dream must die. It is not the dream that needs to die, it's the worldly mindset and selfishness that needs to die. If you have abandoned a dream, no matter how long it has been, pick it up again and embrace the process of fulfillment. He wants to make you into the person that can successfully carry the fulfillment of those dreams.

There is a way to get to the promise and it is not through our way but through heaven's way—which looks a whole lot different. Jesus showed us how to gain the keys to the kingdom but we have been shaped by our culture in such a way that it is difficult to see them. A good model of dying in order to fulfill God's promise is found in the story of Joseph.

In his youth God gave Joseph a dream. He tried to accomplish it the wrong way, by telling his brothers how "great" he was going to be—not a smart move. He then spent the necessary years dying to all that he thought his dream was about. What he thought was a dead end was actually God positioning him like a diamond in a gold setting. He would later be in the perfect position to save the entire race of his people. Through unjust suffering, Joseph was positioned physically, emotionally and spiritually to see God's promises realized. In the early years Joseph did not realize that the dream meant that he would be a "servant" in saving the nation of Israel. The dream looked like it meant a great position—and to the un-renewed mind becoming Pharaoh's right-hand man was indeed a great position, but from heaven's perspective it was a position of service. If Joseph would have retained the same attitude he started out with, he would not have seen God's plan in the whole thing. However his heart was humbled by a series of deaths through difficult circumstances. When the time came he was ready to fulfill God's purposes. God needed his heart, his mind and his values to match heaven so that when the dream came to pass, Joseph would serve his brothers with the authority he had gained instead of using his position to get revenge. Joseph faced many choices before he was able to see his dream come to pass. He had plenty of opportunities to be offended at God by wrong–suffering. He had no choice about remaining in jail, but he could have easily abandoned his trust in God. How many times do we run from hard situations and in doing so, run from the very thing that will position us to fulfill our dreams?

I suggest allowing your authority figures to reveal your heart. God has placed them there as a gift, to reveal things that keep you bound. These things would not be revealed if you were the top dog. I am saddened by those who leave the church too soon. They do not see eye to eye with their leadership so they look for a church that better suits their goals. I see too many miss new levels of freedom by not embracing submission in the midst of conflict. After a few years eager to serve, many associate pastors become spiritual teenagers. When teenagers gain some insight into the world, they begin to have their own ideas about life. Some even think that their parents do not know anything and they cease to listen to them. This is what I see with young leaders. They begin to get their own vision from God and think that they do not need their spiritual parents. The senior pastor all of a sudden becomes 'old school' or 'he doesn't get it.' Then these leaders, with a deep passion and lack of patience, leave too early. They leave behind the spiritual inheritance that comes through honor and miss out on the preparation God wanted to do. Promotions come from working through problems, not running from them. It is too painful for most to submit, so they bail out before the process is complete—and therefore miss out on the blessing. Not only the blessing of spiritual inheritance, but the blessing of a purified heart.

I want to be like Daniel, who while serving a wicked king, honored that king wholeheartedly. When king Nebuchadnezzar had a vision of a sentence of judgment pronounced by an angel, Daniel could have easily said to himself, "Finally! He is going to get what he deserves. I don't have to deal with this guy's bad choices anymore. I don't have to be stuck in this godless kingdom any longer!" Which is often the same spirit we partner with. Instead, Daniel said, *"My lord, if only the dream applied to those who hate you and its interpretation to your adversaries!"* Daniel 4:19. Daniel passed the test of honor and God was able to exalt him and give him profound revelations.

God has placed a dream within you. Making it come to pass is not the hard part, because God knows how to place people in positions of influence. The difficult part is getting our hearts and minds to match heaven so that we will make the right decisions when we get there. The process of dying is the pathway to becoming like Jesus, and we will prosper when we embrace it. Too many have abandoned their dreams prematurely because of impatience. This impatience is usually tied to a fear that, "if I stay under this leadership, my dreams will not be realized. I am wasting time here. I need to move on. God would want me to move on, right? I mean, He has called me to something else." We can justify that our motives for moving on are about God, but if you have had any of these thoughts, the root of this type of thinking is selfish ambition. As long as we see our call higher than serving people, then we will use people to fulfill our call.

Patience

If we want to be free from the world's ambition trap, we must embrace the virtue of patience. *"And let endurance (patience) have its perfect result, so that you may be perfect and complete, lacking in nothing."* James 1:4. The reason patience must have its perfect result in you, is because it cleans out the unhealthy ambition that is driving our poor decisions. It chokes out the world's definition of success in us.

Jesus modeled this patience. His attitude was to wait on the Father's timing. A great example is His first miracle in Cana. He was hesitant and even resistant to his mother asking Him to do a miracle. In John 2:4, Jesus said to her, *"Woman, what does that have to do with us? My hour has not yet come."* Mary and Jesus knew something that everyone around them did not- that He was special, superhuman. Jesus also knew that there was a period of time when He was to reveal what He had been cloaking with humility for thirty years. He expresses to His mother that the present moment was not that time. Jesus eventually consented to His mother and performed His first miracle, the result of this is found in verse 11. *"This beginning of His signs Jesus did in Cana of Galilee, and manifested His glory, and His disciples believed in Him."* This first miracle revealed something that he did not wish to reveal just yet: His glory, or brightness. This sign manifested or made visible to everyone who was paying attention who He was on the inside. From then on, He was a wanted man.

If Jesus should be our example in all things, we should take this example to heart as well. He did not want to be in public ministry before the right time. So often we want to dive right in and even pray prayers of rush. We often disclose to anyone who will listen how great we are or what we have accomplished. If there is a conversation we want to be the one with the most intelligent answer. We are so quick to reveal our brightness. This is not humility nor is this the way of Jesus. He hid Himself until it was necessary. He was reluctant to reveal His glory. Those who cannot wait to dive into significance usually do not see themselves complete without it. When we exercise patience, God is able to mature us. Another word for mature is complete. So the very thing that we think we need to complete us is found in the waiting!

7. TIMING, PREPARATION AND PATIENCE

Once I know what God has called me to, I want so badly to start right away! It is difficult to wait for the right timing, because to me, the right timing is always "as soon as possible." This tendency is probably why God does not tell me everything He has planned for me to do. He knows that I could spoil the plan by executing it at the wrong time.

Before Jesus made wine from water at the wedding in Cana, His mother brought the problem to Him and His response to her was interesting. He said to her that His time had not yet come. This mindset of Jesus is so different from our own. If we truly want to be like Jesus, if God is making us into the image of His Son, then we ought to take notice of His complete nature, even those things that are not so obvious. Jesus did not want to start something before its appointed time. What was Jesus thinking? What was He waiting for? Jesus knew that He was being groomed for a specific purpose, but He also knew that there was something detrimental to starting

His public ministry too early. Maybe He realized that once something was started, it could not be stopped.

So often our desire is to get our ministry started as soon as possible. When receive a promise we ask for it to be fulfilled right away. We ask, "Put me on stage, speak through me, let Your miracles flow through me today!" We take steps toward its fulfillment without considering our much-needed preparation and the consequences of starting something before its time. At the end of my first semester at seminary, my Greek professor gave us this humorous warning: "Now don't go off trying to use this stuff to teach. You only know enough to be dangerous!" My professor was warning us that if we tried to interpret the Greek manuscripts with the little Greek that we knew, we would come to some heretical conclusions. We all know too well of doctrines that have come from a lack of maturity, he did not want more floating around from a bunch of immature Bible students.

One of the notice boards at my seminary was always filled with announcements of churches looking for senior pastors, and students ready to graduate looking for positions. It was like classified ads for new pastors. I always thought it was odd, and even more so now, a person could think that because they have four years of Bible education under their belt that they were ready to pastor a congregation. Pastoring a congregation is a lot more involved than having Bible knowledge. Leading a church or ministry puts pressure on your entire life, not only a person's teaching abilities. Time management, learning to deal with people's expectations and comforting people in their pain are just a few examples of skills that are not often taught in Bible college. Throw on top of it a new marriage or baby and that could be a recipe for disaster. New pastors usually have a break down in their relationship with their spouse and with their relationship with God in the first couple of years. I've seen it happen many times.

Now do you understand why Jesus was not anxious to start his public ministry? My eyes were opened when I read a biography about William Branham. The book *Supernatural: The Life of William Branham* tells the story of a man who received the gift of healing. This gift was so powerful that just about everyone Branham prayed for was healed. In the mid-1900s the word got out and his meetings were packed. He would pray for people until he slumped over with physical exhaustion. When he was driven home around 2:00am or 3:00am in the morning, there were hundreds of people waiting on his front lawn and on his street. Branham could not even eat his breakfast in peace because his heart broke for the desperate and literally dying right outside his door. Who could blame them? If one of my loved ones were dying I would wait outside as well!

When we ask for God to use us in a mighty way, do we know what we are asking for? Branham's life and family were just about destroyed because of this amazing gift of healing. The demand on his life was more than one man could bear. Learning about this man's life coupled with Jesus being hesitant to reveal His glory gave me a new appreciation for God's timing in my life. In God's mercy He vetoes prayers because He knows that the answer to some of our prayers would literally destroy our lives.

Jesus knew that timing and preparation were important. We will do well when we have that same mindset. Those that are mature always check with the Father before leading any public ministry. If one decision leads to another, the timing of one small decision has the potential to affect a chain of events. We could be going after the very thing that God has called us to but because we started too early miss the key preparation and opportunities that were necessary to complete the task. We might even miss important relationships that will be needed for the calling on our lives. God may be waiting for marriages or children to be stronger. Problems and pain can be avoided by waiting on God's timing.

Preparation is key in being used by God. The easy part for God is pouring out His Spirit supernaturally. It is a simple task for God to give words of knowledge, divine revelation or healing through a person. The hard part is getting a person to take on the servant heart of Jesus! If *you* have been asking why God is taking so long to raise you up, He might be waiting for you. He may be developing in your character the strength to withstand the pressures of ministry.

If small and petty things still get between us and our spouse, then being exalted by God may further strain that relationship. Not only does being in a place of influence increase the demand on our time and energy, but also we become a bigger target to the enemy. When politicians run for office, their opponents will dig up anything and everything to destroy their character or reputation. If you really want to know the state of a person's character, put them in the limelight and watch as everything hidden comes to the surface. Outside pressures always magnify the issues of the heart. It is easy to appear like the perfect family, just get a good backdrop and make everyone smile for a photo. The true miracle is uniting a family or an organization to such a degree that they are unbreakable.

If God would have put Joseph in power before he had worked wisdom and humility into him, Joseph might have taken revenge on his brothers when he got the chance. He did not use any wisdom or humility when sharing his dreams with his brothers, but by the time his dream was fulfilled, he displayed them both. He was undertaking his duties as Pharaoh's right-hand man in a wise manner, and it was with great humility that he told his brothers, you didn't put me here, God did it to serve you. *"Don't be afraid. Am I in the place of God? You intended to harm me, but God intended it for good to accomplish what is now being done, the saving of many lives." Genesis 50:19-20*. Joseph's character and ability to handle the situation were a result of the finished work of preparation.

David spent almost fourteen years between being anointed as king and being put into office. On the other hand, Saul did not have the opportunity to be groomed for kingship. He was crowned without preparation, and it did not end well. The preparation and the process are key for an effective and successful ministry, just as the foundation of a building is necessary for its stability. We must not be in a rush to be raised up, but instead, be dependent on the Lord's wisdom for timing. When you have this trust in God's timing, there is no limit to how high God can raise you up. And by the way, God loves to raise His people up!

There are those that think in order to advance the kingdom of God that the Christians must climb to the top of their sphere of influence, business or field of expertise. Then they will be able to influence all those under their supervision. The thought is that with a title, we will be able to create positive moral change and be able to speak into people's lives regarding the gospel. That's a great idea if we are seeing things from an earthly perspective, but from heaven's perspective the Christian's strength has always come from a place of servant hood.

What if God has not created you for that position? What if the person in that position was gifted by God for that position but they just need to become a Christian so that *they* can be influential?! Yes, God wants us the whole earth to be full of the knowledge of Him. However, our methodology may be ineffective if God has created someone else to do the job that we are trying to take over. If you believe that God has created every human being for a purpose, then the world will not be a better place with you in the wrong position. God has made every person to bear an amount of responsibility in the world. There are people flourishing in their field because they are functioning in their gifting. People that are not Christians are causing science to expand, they are causing business and industry to flourish and displaying brilliant leadership. Do we shove them aside so that the Christians can shine? Instead of taking positions from capable people in order to bring in Christian values, we ought to disciple them into what God has made them for: to be the best person they can possibly be. True influence does not need a title.

Every person has influence over a small amount of the earth, just as parents have responsibility over the children that have been entrusted with. We think of taking responsibility from "sinners" so that we can push our morality on the world through control. In Ephesians 6 Paul reminds us that the battle is not against flesh and blood. In other words, our fight is not against people, but against heavenly powers. God's commission is for all of humanity to take the earth from the enemy of our souls. What if every person was discipled so that their sphere of responsibility is stamped with heaven's values? If we can accomplish this, all of the earth will be changed, and the right people will be in the right places! Then we would fulfill Jesus' command, to disciple the nations.

How this looks on a practical level is to speak words of life over everyone we meet. We do not want their position if they will do a better job than us, but we want them to be the best human they can be. We want people to walk fully in their God-given destiny. In case you think I don not care about their salvation, let me say this: by definition the best way to live is to love and follow Jesus. If we take a posture like so many have in the Bible—Joseph, Daniel, Nehemiah, and so many others—our bosses will not be threatened by us. They will know that we do not want their position but on the contrary that we want them to excel in their position! And since that is so unlike the earthly mindset, they just might want to know why.

Just like Daniel, who honored and respected a wicked king, we will be exalted when we serve those who oversee us. This is the way heaven thinks. This is the mind of Christ. We will seek to use our lives to benefit the lives of others, and we will spend our time and energy in propelling them into an abundant life. After all, is that not what Jesus has done for us?

CONCLUSION

God is looking for people He can trust with divine influence. Jesus still wants to make disciples of all nations. He wants to extend His kingdom in the minds and hearts of people throughout the globe. David was a good example of these qualities. God knew that His values would be extended in Israel through David because David had a heart that resembled the heart of God. He saw himself as a conduit that connected the blessings of God to the people of Israel. *"And David realized that the Lord had established him as king over Israel, and that his kingdom was highly exalted, for the sake of His people Israel."* 1 Chronicles 14:2. David recognized that all his influence, all of his power, wisdom and resources was for a purpose. This purpose was not to bless himself. All of it, even the children that God gave to him, were for the purpose of blessing a people, the nation of Israel. The abundant blessings positioned him to bless others. It was because of this attitude that God chose to pour out His abundance on King David.

We all have been blessed with something. The question is, were the blessings meant to stop with us or extend to those around us? We are God's Body on the earth. We have the ability to extend His love to our families, neighborhoods and cities. This was the plan of God from the beginning. As God promised Abraham that he would have as many descendant as the stars, the ultimate goal was that through him *all the nations would be blessed*. May the nations be blessed through us as we function as an extension of the Kingdom of Heaven.

The ultimate cause is the cause of Christ. He is the head of the church and we are His Body. Our daily orders come from the One who laid His life down for us. He made disciples and instructed His disciples to make disciples. That is where we come in. We have a rich heritage of people who have gone before us and passed us the torch. If we are true disciples of Christ then our lives will take on the shape of His. Our ministries will look like His. The very way we think will take on the nature of Jesus.

"Therefore if there is any encouragement in Christ, if there is any consolation of love, if there is any fellowship of the Spirit, if any affection and compassion,

make my joy complete by being of the same mind, maintaining the same love, united in spirit, intent on one purpose. Do nothing from selfishness or empty conceit, but with humility of mind regard one another as more important than yourselves; do not merely look out for your own personal interests, but also for the interests of others. Have this attitude in yourselves which was also in Christ Jesus, who, although He existed in the form of God, did not regard equality with God a thing to be grasped, but emptied Himself, taking the form of a bond-servant, and being made in the likeness of men. Being found in appearance as a man, He humbled Himself by becoming obedient to the point of death, even death on a cross. For this reason also, God highly exalted Him, and bestowed on Him the name which is above every name, so that at the name of Jesus every knee will bow, of those who are in heaven and on earth and under the earth, and that every tongue will confess that Jesus Christ is Lord, to the glory of God the Father." Philippians 2:1-11.

Made in the USA
San Bernardino, CA
01 January 2015